Our Baby

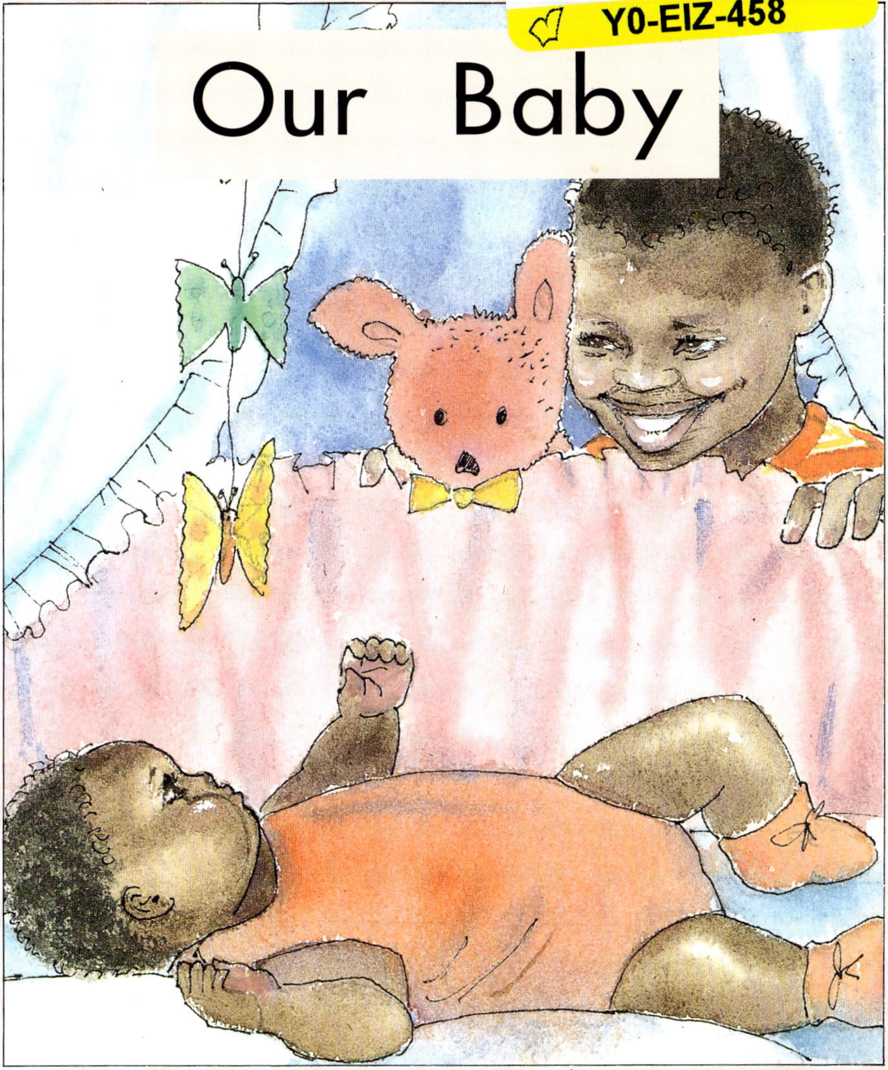

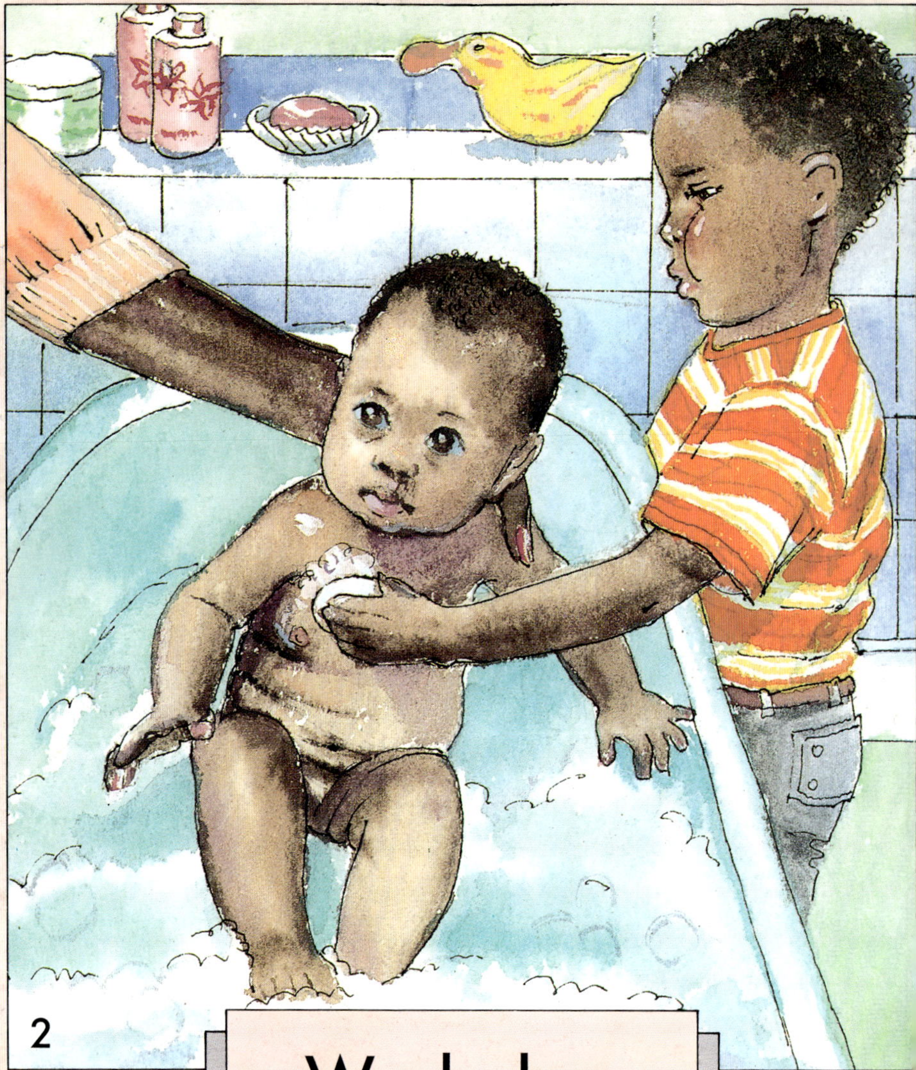

Wash her.

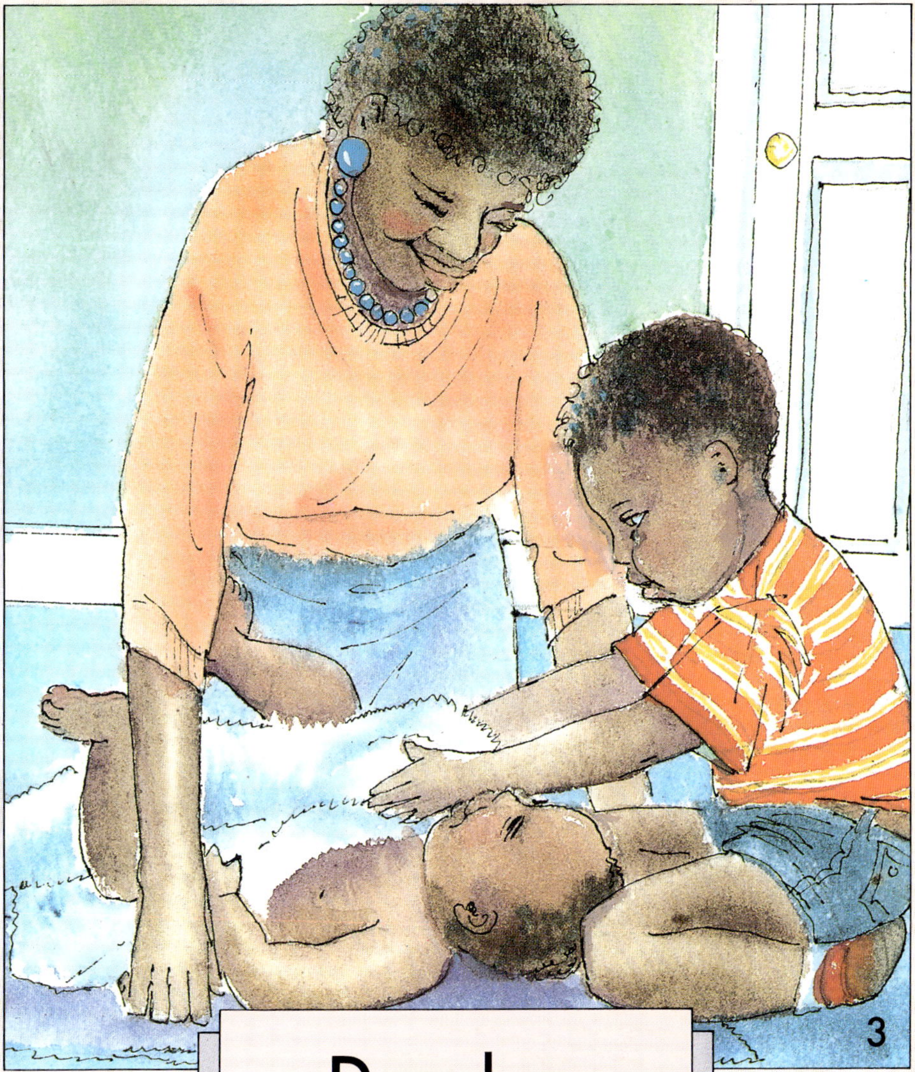

Dry her.

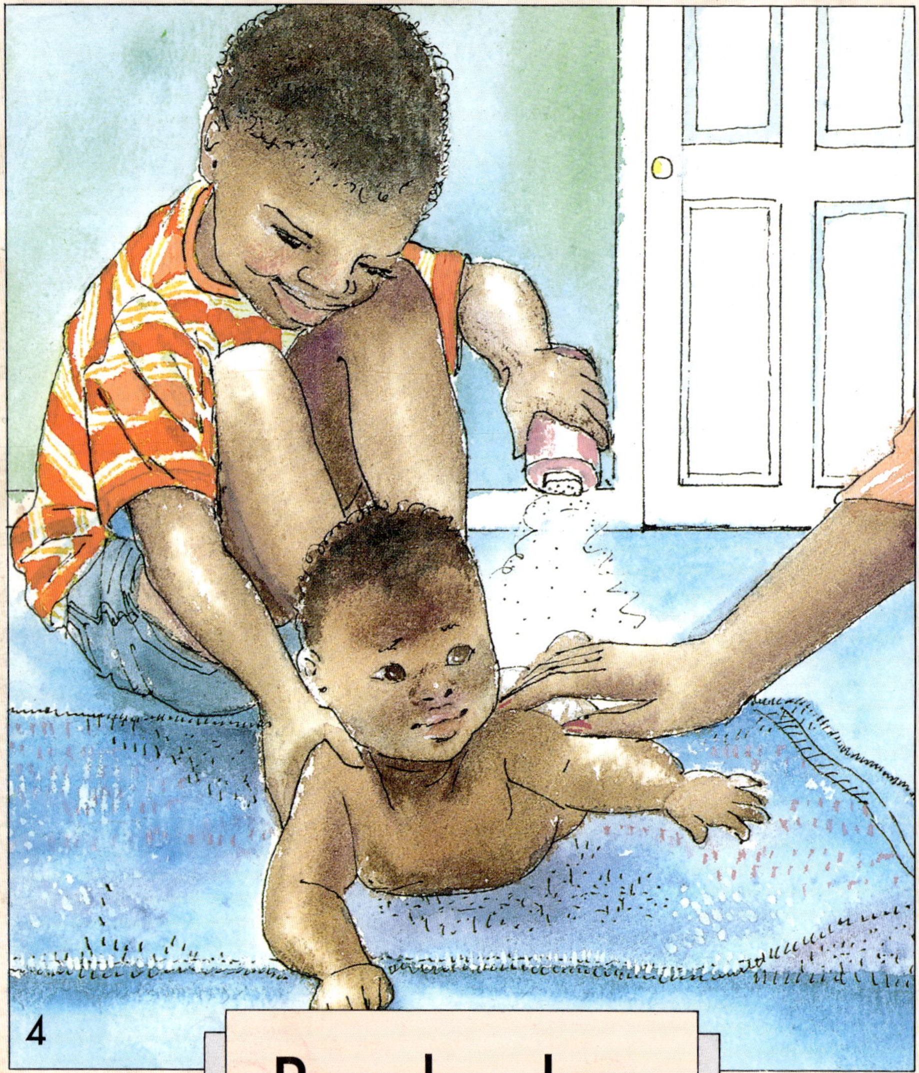

Powder her.

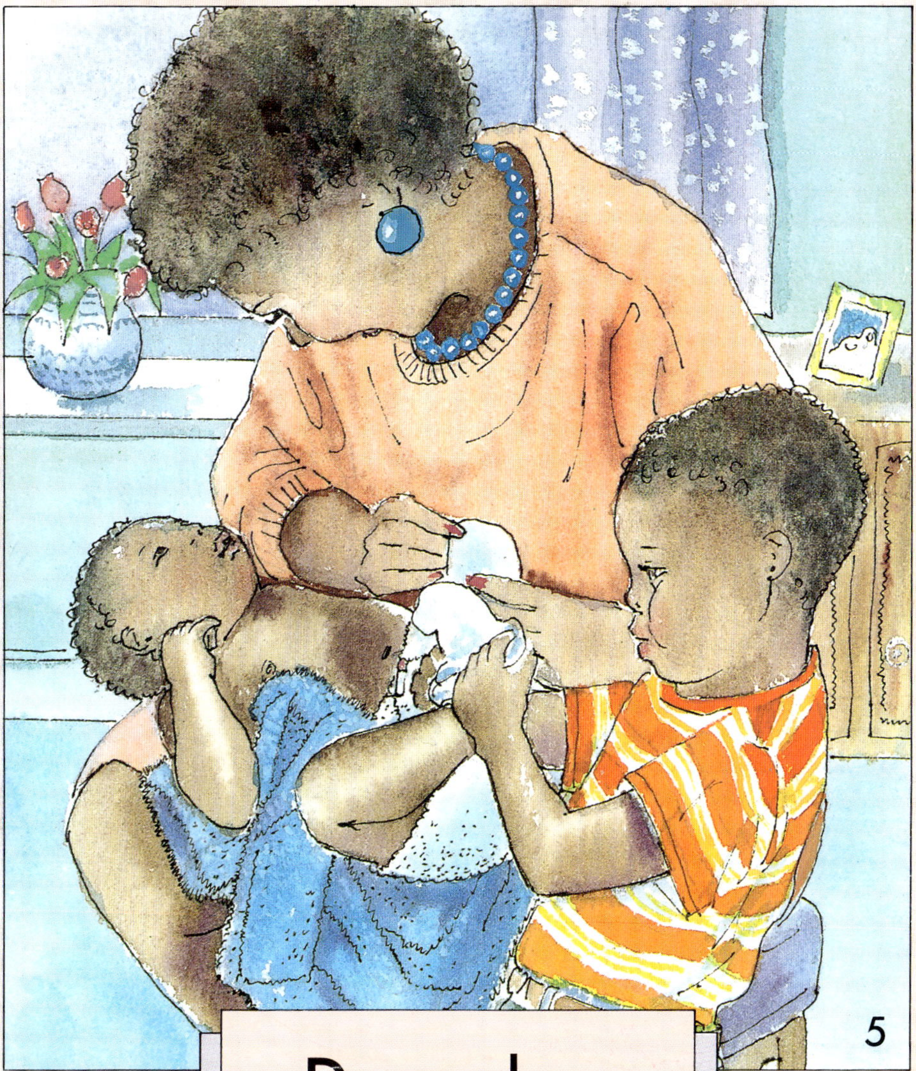

Dress her.

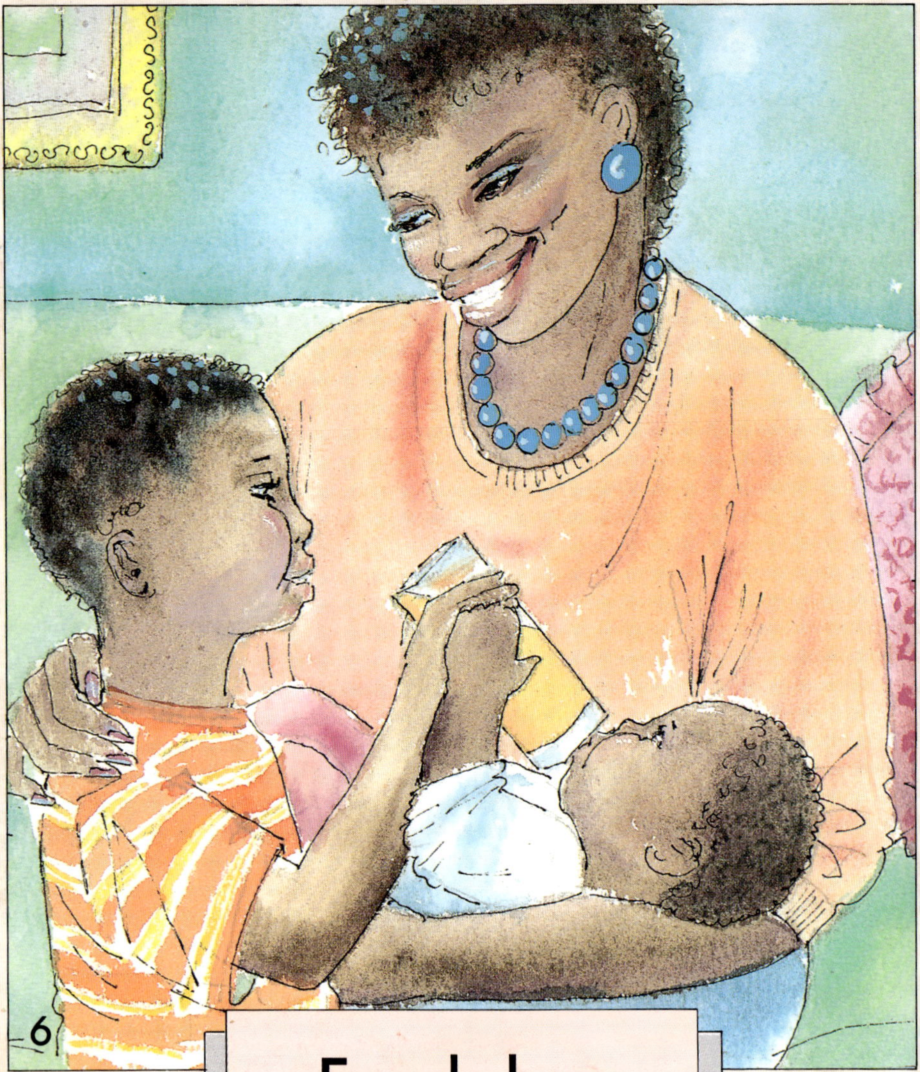

Feed her.

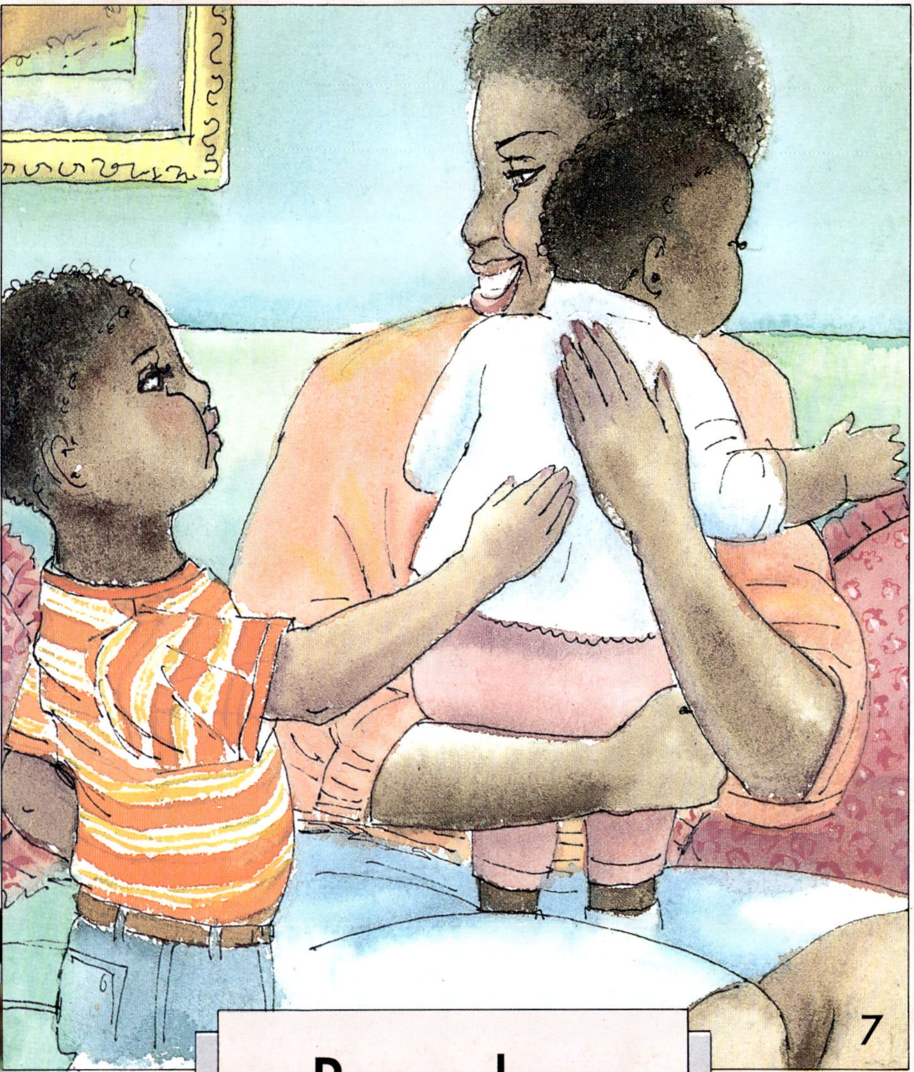

Burp her.

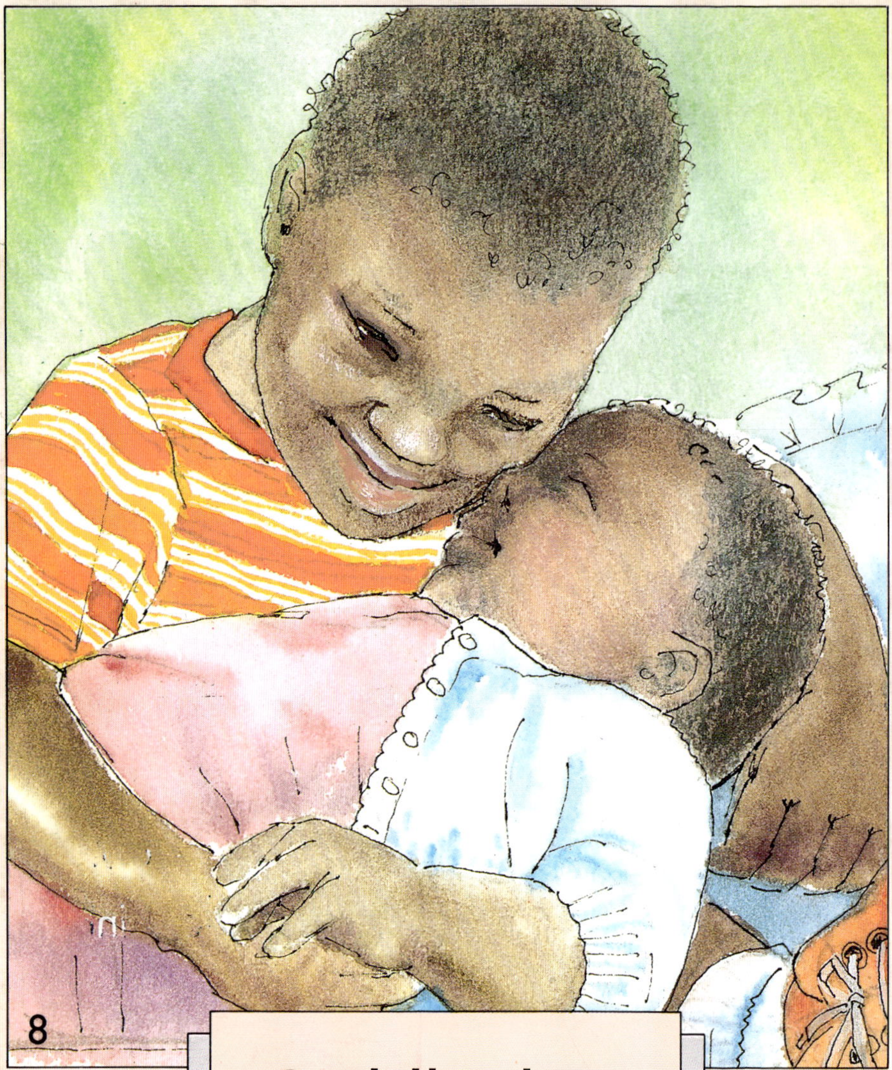

Cuddle her.